AN UNLOVED GUY'S GUIDE

How to Deal

John Logan

JASMINE
HEALTH
Wellness • Diet • Cooking

Library of Congress Cataloging-in-Publication Data

Logan, John.
  [Guys' guide to love]
  An unloved guy's guide : how to deal / John Logan.
    pages cm. — (A guy's guide)
  Originally published in 2008 as the author's A guys' guide to love.
  Includes bibliographical references and index.
  Summary: "Explores the emotion of love in young men and the best ways to deal with crushes, dating, relationships, and breakups. Includes real-life examples, quotes, facts, tips, and quizzes"—Provided by publisher.
  ISBN 978-1-62293-020-3 — ISBN 978-1-62293-021-0 (pbk.) — ISBN 978-1-62293-022-7 (ePUB) — ISBN 978-1-62293-023-4 (PDF) — ISBN 978-1-62293-024-1 (PDF) 1. Interpersonal relations in adolescence. 2. Emotions in adolescence. 3. Teenage boys—Psychology. 4. Love. I. Title.
  BF724.3.I58L64 2014
  155.5'32—dc23
                  2013015762

Future editions:
Paperback ISBN: 978-1-62293-021-0   EPUB ISBN: 978-1-62293-022-7
Single-User PDF ISBN: 978-1-62293-023-4   Multi-User PDF ISBN: 978-1-62293-024-1

Printed in the United States of America
072014 HF Group, North Manchester, IN
10 9 8 7 6 5 4 3 2 1

To Our Readers: We have done our best to make sure all Internet addresses in this book were active and appropriate when we went to press. However, the author and the publisher have no control over and assume no liability for the material available on those Internet sites or on other Web sites they may link to. Any comments or suggestions can be sent by e-mail to comments@enslow.com or to the address below.

Jasmine Health
Box 398, 40 Industrial Road
Berkeley Heights, NJ 07922
USA
www.jasminehealth.com

Illustration Credits: Shutterstock.com: Cory Thoman (brainstorm graphic), pp. 16, 51; freesoulproduction (thumbtack graphic), pp. 5, 7, 11, 41, 50, 56, 60; NLshop (therapy graphic), pp. 14, 15, 18, 19, 24, 26, 27, 28, 29, 34, 37, 40, 46, 57, 58, 61; Paul Matthew Photography, p. 1; vectorgirl (lightbulb graphic), pp. 9, 38, 52; zayats-and-zayats (quotation graphic), pp. 13, 22, 23, 33, 39, 44, 55.

Cover Photo: Paul Matthew Photography/Shutterstock.com

This book was originally published in 2009 as *A Guys' Guide to Love.*

CONTENTS

CHAPTER ONE

This Thing Called Love

Greg and Kaela have lived next door to each other since he moved into the neighborhood, when he was five years old. They had been good friends forever, it seems. But one day a few weeks ago, Greg realized that Kaela meant much more to him than just a friend. All of a sudden, he realized that he wanted to spend more time with her and see her more often. He had always known that there was a special bond between them, but this was something different. He had never felt this way about anyone before.

Among the most important aspects of your life are your **relationships with others.** Friendship is a relationship in which you can feel relaxed and comfortable. But sometimes a friendship becomes something more. It can be confusing, exciting, frustrating, and complicated. All these feelings can be an important part of love.

You and Your Emotions

A part of everyone's personality, emotions are a powerful driving force in life. They are hard to define and understand. But what is known is that emotions—which include anger, fear, love, joy, jealousy, and hate—are a normal part of the human system. They are responses to situations and events that trigger bodily changes, motivating you to take some kind of action.

Some studies show that the brain relies more on emotions than on intellect in learning and in making decisions. Being able to identify and understand the emotions in yourself and in others can help you in your relationships with family, friends, and others throughout your life.

Like Greg, you may be finding yourself attracted to a girl whom you have known for a long time. But for reasons that you can't explain, you now feel there is something different about her. All of a sudden, you want to learn all kinds of things about her that you didn't care about before, such as her favorite color, TV shows, and movies. You're curious about what she likes to do in her spare time, what she does with her friends, and just about anything else about her.

Along with these desires of wanting to know her better come fears. You may be afraid of her reaction if she finds out that you feel this way. It can be really embarrassing if she doesn't feel the same way or if she rejects you. Or maybe you're scared that she does feel the same way—and you don't want to mess things up by saying the wrong thing.

When you're feeling attracted to someone, you can undergo an overload of powerful emotions. And that can be hard to deal with. But try to relax. Keep in mind that your peers—your friends and classmates—are going through the same thing. In fact, most people you know—even your parents—have had similar experiences. They've survived and you will, too!

Understanding yourself. Just take a deep breath, and think about what's going on right now in your life. Things are probably pretty stressful. After all, all kinds of changes are happening to you right now—both in your body and in your mind. You're about to deal with or may already be dealing with puberty—the stage of life when your body matures and changes into that of an adult.

In boys, puberty occurs between the ages of ten and fifteen. It is a time of rapid growth and physical change. You and other guys grow taller, get heavier, and develop more muscles. Your voice gets deeper, and hair starts sprouting on your chin. These changes take place at different rates for different guys. But it is common for guys to be feeling uncomfortable at times as certain body parts are growing and changing shape.

The rapid growth that occurs during puberty is due to increasing amounts of hormones in your body. Hormones are chemical substances that carry messages regulating the activity of cells. In boys,

The Chemicals of Love

While love is most commonly associated with the heart, most of the real action is in the brain. Studies have shown that when a person has strong feelings toward someone else, the brain releases increased amounts of certain chemicals called neurotransmitters. One of these neurotransmitters is dopamine. High levels of dopamine are associated with feelings of interest and excitement.

Being exposed to exciting new things can also trigger the release of dopamine in the brain. So if you take your date on some wild rides at the amusement park, it's likely you'll have a second date with that person. The dopamine released during an exhilarating rollercoaster ride, for example, can also stimulate feelings of attraction.

increased amounts of the hormone testosterone cause changes and growth that are part of becoming a man.

But these changing hormone levels don't affect just your body. They also affect your emotions. As the amounts of hormones in your body change, you can feel emotional upheavals and experience extreme mood swings. At times, you may be feeling really moody and irritable. But at other times, you may feel excited and thrilled, like you're on top of the world. That kind of feeling often happens when you feel strongly attracted to someone else. These feelings can be physical, affecting sexual behavior and desire. They can also be emotional, involving a longing for closeness and feeling connected to someone else.

Understanding love. So what exactly are these romantic feelings? What is this thing called love? Trying to understand love can be challenging, but by taking some time to think about what love means to you, you will better understand what is important to you and to the people in your life. You'll also have a better idea about how to keep your relationships strong.

Simply put, love is hard to define. If you asked people in the street what love is, you would probably not get the same answer from any two people. One generally accepted definition is a strong affection for

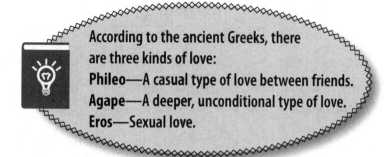

According to the ancient Greeks, there are three kinds of love:
Phileo—A casual type of love between friends.
Agape—A deeper, unconditional type of love.
Eros—Sexual love.

another arising out of kinship or personal ties. That definition basically covers the love you feel for family members and for your friends.

Love of family and friends. A big part of your life is the bond you have with your parents, your brothers and sisters, and friends. The love that you have for and receive from your family members and friends revolves around caring and support. In families with good relationships, this means parents, brothers, and sisters provide emotional support for each other. They take the time to sit down and listen to each other's problems and try to help work out solutions.

A similar kind of support can also come from friends. As you've grown older, you may have noticed that a special bond has developed among you and your best friends. You enjoy spending a lot of time with them. You all may share secrets or jokes that bring you even closer together. And you probably count on your friends being there for you during rough times, just as you will be there for them.

Romantic love. Although the basic elements of caring and support remain the same, the love you feel for family and friends is very different from romantic love. The person you love is someone you believe you can rely on, who will support and be there for you when you need him or her. But in romantic love there is also a physical attraction and an emotional connection. It is a special bond. When song composers, writers, and filmmakers create songs and stories about love, they are usually referring to this intense attraction and romantic relationship between two people.

How and why romantic love develops between any two people is not known. Someone may say he has never felt "in love" even after dating the same person for several months or even years. Another couple may claim they fell in love the first moment they saw each other. And once established, every loving relationship is different. The two people involved are individuals who bring their own values and expectations to the relationship.

Getting to know someone else through a loving relationship can be an exciting and intense time. Depending upon what's going on in the relationship, your feelings when in love can range from the high exhilaration of knowing someone really loves you to the depths of despair during a breakup. You have the opportunity to learn a lot about yourself while developing and sustaining a new relationship, as you make decisions while in the midst of managing powerful emotions. The way you relate to someone close to you can help your relationship change and grow, or it can end it.

Being attracted to someone is the first step on your journey toward discovering what love is all about. Your experiences in a loving relationship will shape you into the kind of person you will become in the future.

Popular Love Stories in Action Films

Lord of the Rings Trilogy: Aragorn, the future king of Gondor, falls in love with the elf maiden Arwen.

Star Wars Trilogy: Han Solo and Princess Leia fall in love in the middle of the Rebellion's struggle against the Empire.

Rocky: The boxer falls in love with the shy and timid store clerk Adrian in the first installment of the Rocky movies. He is tough enough to punch guys in the face and get married.

CHAPTER TWO

A Big Crush

Josh is having trouble concentrating in his classes—at least the ones that Lauren is in. In the lunchroom, he tries to get a seat close enough to Lauren so that he can try to say a few words and make her notice him. But she's one of the most popular girls in school, and Josh doesn't fit in with her group of friends. Still, he knows he really likes Lauren. What can he do?

What Josh is feeling is a crush—an intense feeling of attraction to another person. He doesn't even know Lauren, but he has these strong feelings for her. He'd really like to get to know her better.

Almost everyone, at one time or another, has had a crush. It may simply be an infatuation—an intense, but brief admiration for another person. A crush may not ever lead into anything, particularly if you keep your feelings to yourself. But sometimes a crush can be the beginning of an exciting new relationship.

Crushes usually just happen. Suddenly you realize that you really like the way she smiles, or the direct

"That's why they call them crushes. If they were easy, they'd call them something else."
—from the 1984 film *Sixteen Candles*

way she stares into your eyes. You find yourself daydreaming about your crush, imagining what you would say during a conversation with her in the hallway at school. Or you might think about being on a date together.

But if you spend no time with the girl you have a crush on, there is no chance of your daydream becoming anything more than something in your imagination. Your crush exists as an idea in your head; it is nothing else. Still, the feelings associated with having a crush can be similar to feeling like you're in love. But it is unlikely that someone who has never spoken to you will fall in love with you!

When you have a crush on someone, you have choices. You can do nothing, keep your feelings to

Ways to Get to Know Your Crush

- Have an online chat
- Pass a note
- Talk on the phone
- Have a face-to-face conversation

yourself, and hope that you eventually get over her. Or you can take a chance and do something about your feelings. Most likely you'll feel pretty nervous about what she'll say or do. But if you don't take the chance, you'll never know what her response would have been.

If you decide to let her know you're interested. If you don't know your crush at all, try to become friends first. Start talking to her. Invite her to join a group of friends who are going to the school basketball game. Figure out what common interests you have. For example, if you like listening to the same music or share the same subjects in school, you'll probably find you have plenty to talk about.

If you have a few conversations with a girl before you ask her out, chances are you will be more successful when you do ask her out. If she doesn't know you at all, she may be startled by your invitation. All she'll have to go on is her first impression and the way you look—which may or may not work to your advantage.

Getting to know someone as a friend first can often be rewarding. Conversations between the two of you can be easier. And knowing what the other likes to do for fun will help if dating is something you have in mind for the future. And if things don't work out in a romantic relationship, it is possible to go back to being friends if both of you are okay with that.

If she's not interested in you. You've tried every trick in the book—carrying her books, walking her to

Crush Confusion

Crushes can be confusing, but when you have a crush on someone you are learning about yourself and the kind of person you feel attracted to. You may find you have a crush on a girl or another guy. Such feelings are okay and normal. However, if you feel confused or worried about your feelings, you should talk to a trusted adult such as a parent or other family member, your doctor, or a school counselor.

Does This Crush Have a Chance?

1. Have you had a conversation with this girl in school?

2. Does she know your name?

3. Do you have any classes with her?

4. Have you ever seen her outside of school?

5. If you answered yes to question 4, did you have a conversation?

6. Do you know how she likes to spend her time?

7. Have you ever talked to her on the phone?

8. Does she come up to you in the hallway to say hello?

Give yourself one point for every "yes."
0–2 = *Not a chance*
3–5 = *Maybe*
6–8 = *It's looking good*

class, holding her spot in the lunch line—and she still won't go out with you. So what do you do?

You could simply try to forget about your crush and move on. Or you could settle for just being her friend. But be honest with yourself and with her— if your feelings for her are more than those of just a friend and she doesn't feel the same way, you probably should not hang around with her until you feel like you can be "just friends."

Another option is to be patient and bide your time. Try inviting her to some activities involving a group of your friends. This way, she'll have a chance to get to know you and accept a date once she knows you better. Or maybe you'll find you're no longer interested. But if you are still interested, ask her out again. Just because she said no once doesn't mean she'll say no the second or third time. However, there is a difference between a determined pursuer and a stalker. If she's already told you to stay out of her way, it's unlikely she'll change her mind about going out with you. Respect her decision and leave her alone.

Some of the time, you will ask a girl out and get flat-out rejected. If she says no, it hurts—a lot. But try to remember, these things happen to people all the time. Being rejected is not the end of the world. To rebound, call some of your guy friends to join in

Getting To Know Her . . . Online?

Social networking Web sites such as MySpace and Facebook provide the technology that allows you to make friends around the world. But remember, when you post information online you are making that information available for the whole world to see. If you think certain things should be private, don't put them on the Internet. Strangers might use that information to steal your identity, hack your computer, or even stalk you. Other Internet safety tips include:

- Be extremely careful about talking to and flirting with people you don't know. Some people using the Internet include false information, and they pretend to be someone they are not.

- Restrict access to your Web site to the people you know.

- Don't post your full name, address, phone number, and other private information.

- Remember, once you post information, it may remain available anyway. Others may have saved it to their computers and they can repost it again even if you take it down.

- Be wary of meeting people you've met online in person. If you decide to, meet in a public place during the day with friends. Tell an adult what you are doing before you go. Make sure that person knows where you're going and when you'll be back.

- If you feel threatened by or uncomfortable about something posted about you or someone you know, tell your parents or another adult you trust. Report it to the police and to the social networking site.

Adapted from "Facts for Consumers: Social Networking Sites: Safety Tips for Tweens and Teens," Federal Trade Commission, May 2006

What Are My Options?

A. Go for it! If your crush is on a classmate, try to hang out with her as a friend. Once you start spending time around her, your feelings and ideas will become much clearer. If a romantic relationship doesn't work out, at least you'll get a new friend.

B. Forget about it! If the crush is unrealistic (like on a celebrity you'll never meet) or if you don't feel ready for a relationship, try to get the person off your mind. Spend your time on a new hobby or sport with your friends.

C. Talk about it. Pull aside one of your friends and tell him or her what is on your mind. Ask your friend for an opinion or advice about what to do. Make sure you confide in a close friend, who won't tell others about your situation. And if you're the one being confided in, don't gossip about your friend's crush.

some activities that will keep your mind off of what happened. Play video games, watch a movie, play basketball or football, or listen to your favorite album.

At some point in time, you'll find yourself interested in a different girl. And she may be the one who gives you the answer you want to hear. Even if you are unsuccessful, it isn't the worst thing in the world to be friends.

CHAPTER THREE

First Dates

Brad finally got the courage up to ask Jackie out and she said yes. Now he is worried about what will happen next. Will she like him? Where should they go? A movie is a possibility, and maybe dinner before that. Brad's really worried. What if she doesn't have a good time hanging out with him? Will they ever talk again? He feels unsure of himself and uncertain about what he's gotten into.

Are you ready to start dating? There is really no right time or age when people should start dating. It varies from person to person. Some people have relationships without going out on formal dates, that is, dates with just the two of you. In fact, you may really care about someone whom you see mostly at school or while hanging out with other friends.

Family rules. Actually, the decision to go out on a formal date may not be entirely up to you. Some parents may forbid their kids from dating until they reach a certain age. Others may feel their kids are simply not ready yet—or they may feel uncomfortable about a specific person their kid is interested in dating.

This doesn't refer to just her parents. Your folks may not be comfortable with the idea of you dating, either. If that is the case, you may need to take some steps to earn their support. The best way to do that is to show that you are a responsible person in other areas. If your parents ask you to take care of certain chores, make sure you get them done on time and without an argument.

In the same way, you'll want to figure out ways to show the parents of the girl you want to date that you can be trusted. If you really like the person and want to date her, try to get to know her parents. At some point, you could ask them why they have those rules.

"Remember that great love and great achievements involve great risk."
—Anonymous

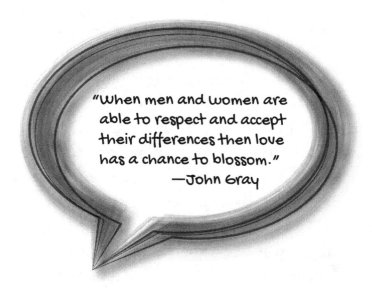

"When men and women are able to respect and accept their differences then love has a chance to blossom."
—John Gray

At the very worst, you might not be able to take her on dates, but if the parents meet you and think well of you, they could eventually change their mind. You may have to simply wait for them to say it's okay for her to date you.

If both sets of parents give the okay for you to date, most likely they will establish some rules. One of the biggest ones is the curfew—the time they set for you to be back home after a date. If you want her parents to approve of you—and not object to any future dates—your best bet is to try to abide by the rules they establish. If they want their daughter home by 11:00 P.M., do your best to make sure that happens—or be ready to explain to her parents what happened that made you arrive at her home at 11:15 P.M. instead.

Similarly, show your parents that you are responsible by abiding by the curfew they set for you. If you don't agree with their restrictions, ask if you can discuss them further. Have a conversation in which you remain calm and polite. Perhaps they can help you understand where they are coming from. At the same time, you can let them know how you feel about the situation. Perhaps they will change your curfew time. But if they don't, make sure you follow their rules. Don't make them worry about you because you're late. If you show them that you can be responsible, they may be willing to talk about making some changes to family rules and curfews in the future.

First Impressions

If you want her parents to think well of you, be sure to make a good first impression. Be attentive and polite when they are talking to you. While meeting the parents can be potentially embarrassing, just keep in mind that her parents want to know who you are because they care about their daughter. And if they don't like you, they can influence her decision about whether to keep dating you.

Recognize that parents set rules on curfews for their daughters—and sons—because they care about their kids. They want to know where they are and have them home at a reasonable hour because they want them to be safe.

How parents can help. Depending on how old you are and whether or not you have a driver's license, you may find that you have to depend on her parents or yours to provide transportation on dates. Most states don't allow kids to get their license until the age of sixteen or older. But if you need a ride and the parents are able, they will probably be happy to help out. Be sure to ask them politely and to give some advance notice, too, if possible.

A 2002 *Teen People* poll notes that 91 percent of teens say they don't like having a parent driving them around on a date. However, when they don't have an alternative way of getting places, most teens appreciate getting a ride from their mother or father.

Parents may also be willing to help you out financially on dates. That is why it helps to be on good terms with your folks and to keep them informed about your dating plans. In fact, they would probably also welcome the chance to meet the girl you like. If they can help out, parents are more likely to offer some cash for you to use on a date if they know your plans.

Another way parents can help is by talking to you about dating and relationships. Take a few minutes to ask for advice or their opinion about the person you are interested in dating. You'll be showing them that you value their advice, and you may also gain some new perspectives.

The first date. First dates can be intimidating, although your comfort level may depend on how well you know your date before asking her out and how

Three Approaches to Try When Asking for a Date

The direct approach: Go up to the girl and just ask, "Will you go out with me?" Simple and easy.

The conversational approach: Start a conversation by talking about things she is interested in or about something that happened in class. During the conversation, slip in a suggestion that you both go to the movies.

The long-term approach: Have several friendly conversations with the girl. Ask her different things. Discuss her interests. Build a casual friendship. Then, when you feel comfortable enough, ask her out on a date.

Adapted from Susan Rabens, *The Complete Idiot's Guide to Dating for Teens* (2001)

When You Ask Her Out

Get to know her first. If asking her out are the first words you have said to her, then chances are you may not be successful.

Have a plan. Know what you are going to say and where the date will be.

Speak clearly. It can be hard to talk when you're feeling nervous, but do you want her to have to ask you to repeat yourself? Don't mumble—make sure you talk so that she can understand you.

Act confident, even if you don't really feel confident. Girls don't want to go out with a guy who seems nervous and unsure of himself.

much time you have already spent together. If you have not had many conversations with the girl until now, you may find it hard to talk in a one-on-one setting.

No matter how well you know her, there's a lot you can do to make a good impression. Be respectful and polite. Open doors, give her compliments, and treat her well.

At the same time, be aware of how she treats you. If she appears to take your attention as something

Some First Date Do's and Don'ts

DO make eye contact. Be sure to look her in the eye while you are talking. It will make it easier for both of you to talk.

DO relax. Take it easy and let the date progress. Don't try to be someone else or to be a comedian (unless you really are one). Act natural.

DO compliment her. Say nice things to her. Compliment her dress and appearance.

DO spontaneous things. Don't be shy about changing plans for your date if an idea pops in your head.

DON'T be pushy. Don't be too physical. A little bit of contact isn't bad, but don't try to hold her hand—or do anything else!—if it makes her uncomfortable.

DON'T talk only about yourself. Get her to talk about herself by asking a lot of questions that keep the conversation moving.

DON'T limit your date. Keep an open mind. If at first she doesn't seem quite what you had in mind, give her a chance. You may be surprised!

DON'T use swear words. There isn't anything more unattractive than a guy who swears a lot.

Adapted from Lindsay, "Ten Do's & Don'ts on a First Date," *Helpingteens.org*, May 19, 2007

Great First Dates

Here are some fun things to do on a first date:

The classic date—The dinner and a movie gig is the go-to first date for a lot of people. However, it can be expensive and require transportation. You can always invite her over to your house for a pizza and a movie that you rented. Make sure it is one that she likes and that she and her parents know that your parents will be home.

The researched date—Talk to her friends and find out some of her interests. If she likes playing a sport, take her somewhere where the two of you can compete. Don't be afraid if she's better than you. After all, fun—not winning—is the point.

The creative date—Think up some fun activities, such as a walk through a local art museum, a hike in the woods, or a game of Frisbee® in the park.

she deserves, but doesn't treat you with any respect in return, you might want to reconsider your interest in her. Similarly, you'll want to notice how she treats other people. Is she rude when you introduce her to the friend you meet at the movie theater? Does she make mean comments about the waitress in the restaurant? The little things that she does on your first date can tell you a lot.

During your date, talk and ask questions. This is your opportunity to learn more about her. You may find that the feelings of attraction that initially drew you to her can fizzle out quickly if you have very little in common. On the other hand, even if you have many differences, you may decide that this makes her very interesting.

Remember, a date is an opportunity to get to know someone better. Don't put unnecessary pressures on yourself or your date. Relax and have fun.

CHAPTER FOUR

The Dating Game

Each night, Tim and Melissa talk on the phone for an hour. Every weekend they go to the movies together, or they meet at each other's houses to watch a DVD together. One day a week, they both volunteer at the animal shelter. Because they live close to each other, they often take walks in the evenings after dinner.

Spending time with a girl gives you the chance to really know her. The more time you spend with her, for example, the better idea you have of what she is like when she is mad, stressed, upset, or happy. You'll know what she likes to do for fun and what dreams and desires she has.

Over time, you may find there are things that you really admire and appreciate in your girlfriend. Or you may find that as you get to know her better, there are certain things that you don't like or approve of. In other words, after a certain period of time, you know enough about yourself and about her to determine if you would like to stay in the relationship.

Things to do. While you're still in the "getting to know you" stage, you don't have to go out on formal dates all the time. You can see each other when you get together with friends or just hang out with each other. Some informal dates can include the following:

- Attend school plays, music program concerts, and sporting events together.
- Put together a basket of food and go for a picnic in the park or in her backyard.
- Go on a walk around the neighborhood. This can give you some privacy and quality time together.
- Teach her a sport you like to play, or ask her to teach you one that she enjoys.
- Or if you don't play sports, think of something else you could work on together. Teach her your favorite video game or work on creating a Web site together.
- Volunteer together at an animal shelter or nursing home.

Who pays? In the beginning of a dating relationship, the person who did the asking out should cover the costs of the date. But after you have been going out together for a while, it's okay to talk about who pays for dates that are expensive. Seeing movies or going to concerts can cost a lot. Let her know if things are getting too expensive for you. Maybe she'll offer to pay for tickets. Make sure you have enough money on

"It doesn't matter if the guy is perfect or the girl is perfect, as long as they are perfect for each other."
—from the 1997 film Good Will Hunting

you to cover likely expenses before you go out on a date.

Make her feel special. If you have been together for a while, you may want to show her that you really appreciate her. There are a lot of little ways you can share your romantic feelings.

You could play music that reminds you both of your first dance together or your first date. A lot of couples will have a special song that they refer to as "Our Song" whenever they hear it played.

When your girlfriend is upset about something, be there to give her a hug and a shoulder to cry on. You don't really need to say anything at all. Just let her know you'll be around when she's feeling down.

Let Her Know You Care

Here are some silly one-liners that will make her smile:

"Are you tired? Because you've been running through my mind all day."

"If I were to rearrange the alphabet, I would put U and I together."

"Help, something's wrong with my eyes! I just can't take mine off you."

"You're like a dictionary—you add meaning to my life!"

"Do you have a map? 'Cause I just got lost in your eyes."

During the year, remember the monthly anniversary of your first date. Write a note, send a card, give her chocolates, or pick some flowers and present her with the bouquet. Make sure not to forget her birthday and the big one-year anniversary.

If she gets sick, come by for a visit with a big get-well card that all your friends signed. You could also bring a big balloon or some flowers. It will make her feel so much better to know that you care.

CHAPTER FIVE

Making Things Work

John and Lindsey have been dating for about six months. After spending a lot of time together, both in and out of school, they have gotten to know each other pretty well. John knows that when Lindsey is stressed out, she will sometimes snap at him. Lindsey sees that John often deals with his problems by ignoring them, and sometimes that includes her. They both realize that these habits are not the best way to deal with each other and are working to try to change.

When you're in love with someone, you do your best to keep your relationship strong. In John and Lindsey's case, they are aware they have some problems with how they sometimes treat each other. However, both are making an effort to do something about it.

A serious relationship is more than sexual attraction. It requires taking a strong interest in the other person. You both need to think about what you need to do to keep things strong. The best relationships—including those with friends and family—involve four important elements: trust, honesty, respect, and good communication.

Trust. An important part of a healthy relationship is being able to trust the other person. That means you both can believe that the other will be reliable. You both consider your commitment to each other to be serious. That means you'll do your best to be there for each other, especially during stressful times. And you'll consider your relationship of major importance. That means neither of you will risk losing it by flirting with other people. If there is a lack of trust between the two of you, your relationship is headed for problems.

Honesty. Related to trust, honesty is essential to any good, healthy relationship. If you aren't telling your girlfriend the truth, then she'll never be able to trust anything you say. Along these lines, don't pretend to be someone you're not or to be interested in certain things that she likes if you really aren't. Of course, you should make an effort to learn about her interests before stating that you don't like them. But if you can't be willing and open to learning about what she likes, perhaps the two of you aren't a good match.

Respect. To respect someone means to pay attention and give value to the feelings, rights, and wishes of that person. In other words, it means treating the other person as you would like to be treated yourself. After you've spent a lot of time with a person, you may find you're taking her for granted. Or worse, you may fall into a habit of teasing or insulting her. No one deserves that kind of treatment. If you can't be respectful in your relationships, you may soon lose them.

Along the same lines, in a relationship with a girl, it is important to respect her wishes when it comes to the physical aspect of love. It is up to you to have respect for her feelings and comfort level. Don't pressure her to do things she wouldn't normally want to do.

Good communication. When you care about someone, you should always strive to share your thoughts. Communicating can mean simply letting each other know your plans for the week, or it can mean talking about why one of you is angry with the other.

Being honest may sound simple, but sometimes it can be hard to practice. You may not want to talk with your girlfriend about what is on your mind and how you are feeling. Most guys have trouble doing that, but do your best to make your honest opinions part of your relationship.

Sometimes issues will come up: She may get jealous that you were talking to another girl, or you may feel jealous of her. She may get angry, thinking you want to hang out with your friends more than with her. Or maybe you're upset that you haven't seen her for a long time because she's been "too busy."

Ingredients for a Successful and Loving Relationship

1. **Attraction** is the "chemistry" part of love. It's all about the physical interest that two people have in each other. Attraction is responsible for the desire you feel to kiss and hold the object of your affection. Attraction is also what's behind the flushed, nervous-but-excited way you feel when that person is near.

2. **Closeness** is the bond that develops when you share thoughts and feelings that you don't share with anyone else. When you have this feeling of closeness with the person you are dating, you feel supported, cared for, understood, and accepted for who you are. Trust is a big part of this.

3. **Commitment** is the promise or decision to stick by the other person through the ups and downs of the relationship.

Adapted from "Love & Romance," *TeensHealth.org*, February 2007

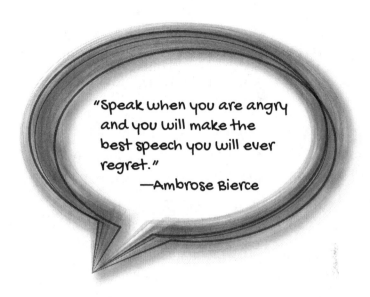

"Speak when you are angry and you will make the best speech you will ever regret."
—Ambrose Bierce

These kinds of situations can lead to serious disagreements that could endanger your relationship. To keep it strong, you both need to try to solve your misunderstandings and conflicts in healthy ways.

This means you need to bring up the problem in a direct way but without placing any blame. Let her know that you think she has been mean to you, or ask if you have done something to upset her. The next step is to talk about how it makes you feel. Does it make you mad that she didn't talk to you all day? Or is she angry that you were out with your friends and didn't call her at all?

Try to be open and not react with anger or other negative emotions when listening to her side of the story. If you are at fault, apologize and try to find out what you can do in order to make it up to her. Say something like, "I'm really sorry about what I did. I didn't know it would make you feel that way."

If you think she did something wrong, choose your words carefully. Let her know how her behavior made you feel: "I felt upset when I didn't hear from you all day because I thought something happened to you." That kind of statement works a lot better in clearing the air than making an angry, accusatory statement like "Why didn't you call?!"

Dinner With the Parents

She invites you over to her house for dinner with her family. A panic comes over you. What do you do? Here are a few tips:

Dress well. Avoid sneakers and sandals. If the weather is cold, wear a good sweater.

Always say "please" and "thank you" when asking for dishes.

Look family members in the eye when you are talking to them.

Be yourself.

Offer to help clear the table or serve dessert.

Make sure you treat your girlfriend well.

Characteristics of a Healthy Relationship

- Strong interest in each other as persons
- Mutual respect
- Trust
- Honesty

- Support
- Fairness and equality
- Separate identities
- Good communication

Adapted from "Am I in a Healthy Relationship?" *TeensHealth.org*, April 2008

Remember, the way you communicate can go a long way to resolving problems. The way you handle your disagreements and arguments says a lot about how much you trust and respect each other.

Always try to solve your problems. Don't ignore or walk away, unless you need a few moments to get a handle on your angry feelings. Dealing with conflicts in a relationship is difficult. However, if you are willing to put time into figuring out how to resolve them, then your relationship will not only survive, but it will grow stronger.

CHAPTER SIX

Your Other Relationships

It was Friday night and Michael had a problem. He was supposed to go to his girlfriend Natalie's house and keep her company while she babysat her little sister. But his friend Nick had just called him to say that the guys were going to the basketball courts to play a pickup game under the lights. Michael's friends gave him a hard time yesterday because he had already spent most of that week hanging out with Natalie. He didn't want to make his friends even madder, but he also knew that Natalie would not be happy if he bailed on her.

Even when you're in a committed relationship, it is important that you don't forget your other relationships. Of course, if you've made a promise to help your girlfriend out with a chore, you need to abide by that promise. But if no promises were made, you shouldn't feel guilty about wanting to do stuff with friends sometimes. And she shouldn't get mad that your parents say you can't go out with her this weekend because they want you to visit your grandmother. After all, other people are a part of your life, too.

Making time for friends. While a romantic relationship can be fun and you can enjoy spending a lot of time with the girl you are dating, you don't need to give her your exclusive attention. Some people have lost friends when dating because they haven't made time for anyone else.

Discovering the balance between time spent with your girlfriend and with your group of friends can be difficult. Both deserve a certain amount of attention. You don't want your friends to be mad at you for spending too much time with your girlfriend. But at the same time, you don't want your girlfriend to be angry that you're always with the guys.

Be aware of the message you're sending when you ignore the group or the girl—one or the other will come to believe the relationship doesn't mean much to you. And think about it. What happens if you and your girlfriend break up? If you have drifted away from your friends, you will have lost an important support group. You need to make sure to maintain a healthy balance between your group of friends and your girlfriend.

Dealing with teasing. Maybe you've started dating earlier than a lot of your friends. Now they're

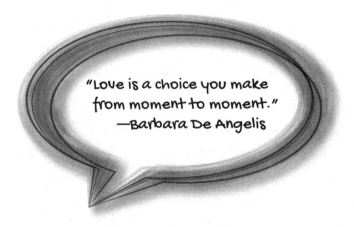

"Love is a choice you make from moment to moment."
—Barbara De Angelis

giving you a hard time when you tell them you're going to watch your girlfriend's basketball game instead of joining them for a video game session.

Do your best to accept that there will be teasing from your friends. Their behavior is normal. They may be envious of you and your relationship. Or in their way, they may be saying they're hurt that you don't want to spend time with them. Whatever is behind their remarks, they are still your friends.

Just smile and do your best to ignore the teasing. But don't distance yourself from friends. Make sure you set aside times when you do things with just them. Invite them over or suggest a pickup game for next weekend. Do your best to keep those relationships alive.

An even more difficult form of teasing may come from your family. Both younger and older brothers and sisters may tease you for being "in love." Or they may do their best to embarrass you in front of your girlfriend.

Teasing from siblings can be harder to deal with than that from friends because you can't always walk away from it. Try not to show it if you feel annoyed. Leave the situation—go to your room or take a walk. Don't let yourself be brought down by their teasing. However, if it gets to be too much, let your mother or father know, and ask for some advice on what to do. It's likely your parents will listen to your complaint and have a talk with the troublemakers.

Making time for family. Parents can sometimes become annoyed when you spend every waking hour with your new love and overlook your responsibilities at home. They may also be concerned if you are never available for family activities.

Avoid these kinds of issues by keeping communication lines open with your mother and father. You can keep your parents happy by letting them know your plans. For example, before you call your girlfriend to say you'll be over on Saturday afternoon, make sure your father knows that you're counting on him to give you a ride. Double check with your mother about when the party for your uncle's fiftieth birthday party is so you don't ask your girl to a movie that night. In

Talk to Your Parents

Discuss the rules ahead of time so you are clear about their expectations.

Follow the rules. If your plans mean you'll be late for curfew, let them know and ask if you can have an exception to the rule.

Pick your battles. Avoid fights over every little thing. If you are going to argue, make sure you deal with the issues that are important to you.

Don't lose your temper. Try to remain calm when your parents say no about something. Listen to what they say.

In a calm voice, ask to explain your side of the issue. Ask your parents to give you the same respect that they want from you.

Accept their decision gracefully, even if it is not the response you wanted.

other words, keep your parents in the loop. Do your best to communicate with them.

If your parents decide you shouldn't date each other. Perhaps her parents just don't like you. Or maybe your parents don't like her, and they forbid you from seeing each other anymore. What do you do?

It is a serious matter when your parents don't like the person you are dating because she is of a different background, race, or religion. A situation like this can be an opportunity to sit down and talk to your parents about what they believe and why they believe it. Even if you feel angry about their attitude, keep a level head and explain why you disagree.

On the other hand, perhaps your parents don't like your new girlfriend because they don't like the way she treats you. Their opinion should cause you to think seriously about the relationship that you are in.

Letting your parents influence your decisions can be hard. But when it comes to a relationship with the opposite sex, what your parents think and want can have a big influence over whether or not you hang out with a specific person. Ask yourself: "Is this girl worth getting into a fight with my parents?"

If you continue seeing this girl despite what your parents say, they will only become angry. You will have broken their trust by sneaking around behind their backs. And a broken trust is hard to repair.

The best thing to do if your parents want you to end a relationship is to sit down with them and have a long discussion. Try to find out their specific reasons. But be willing to compromise—maybe you and the girl in question may only be friends for now. In time, your folks may change their mind. But meanwhile, respect their point of view.

CHAPTER SEVEN

Do the Right Thing

> *Trent and Michelle have been dating for around three months. They hang out all day after school, watch movies together, and see each other for weekend dates. Since Michelle and Trent are going out, she doesn't think he should be having anything to do with other girls. The other day, she saw him talking with Julie, one of his friends from class. Michelle became furious. She cornered Trent later that day and let him know that he shouldn't be talking to other girls.*

Is it love or is it jealousy? Michelle is acting jealous and putting demands on Trent that he doesn't think are fair at all. Her behavior makes him wonder about whether to stay with her.

What do you do when you really care about someone but you don't think the person is treating you right? One of the worst things to do is nothing—thinking that if you just ignore her outbursts, they'll eventually stop. Ignoring a problem won't solve it. When you both don't agree about something, you need to take steps to solve the conflict. That means you need to talk. In Michelle's case, she needs to recognize she has a problem—her jealousy is not a sign of her love. It is a sign of controlling and unhealthy behavior.

When jealousy becomes abuse. When one partner in a relationship is jealous and controlling, things can quickly go from bad to worse. Such problems occur in as many as one out of three teen relationships, some studies show. The vast majority of cases involve the boy being abusive to his girlfriend. This abuse can be controlling behavior in which the guy puts down and constantly criticizes the girl, blames her for his problems, or uses threats of violence or actual violence.

If you have a friend who is in an abusive relationship, try to get help for that person. Talk with someone you trust—a teacher, a guidance counselor, a doctor, a friend, or a parent. You may also want to contact the police or call the domestic violence hotline listed on page 63. If the person wants to stay in the relationship, he or she must realize that the violence will not go away by itself. Counseling or some other form of outside help is necessary.

Just because you feel jealous from time to time doesn't mean you are abusive and controlling. But watch yourself. If you find yourself feeling jealous of your girlfriend, stop and think. Be aware that your jealous feelings are affecting your behavior and the way you treat her. Remember, love means being respectful and caring in a relationship.

Respect her and respect yourself. Respect is a key part of any relationship. In friendships, it means that good friends respect your values and beliefs. They don't tease or put you down because you stand by your choices, like in making decisions about whether to smoke cigarettes or drink alcohol. It is important to resist peer pressure to do things you don't think are right or that you aren't comfortable with.

An Unhealthy Relationship?

You are in an unhealthy relationship if your girlfriend . . .

- Constantly criticizes the way you look or dress.
- Keeps you from seeing friends or from talking to any other guys or girls.
- Wants you to quit an activity, even though you love it, so you can spend more time with her.
- Hits you whenever she's angry.

Adapted from "Am I in a Healthy Relationship?" *TeensHealth.org*, April 2008

Are You Treating Her Right?

Take this quiz to see if you are treating your girlfriend right. Give yourself one point for every "yes" answer and zero points for each "no" answer.

1. Do you get jealous when you see your girlfriend talking to other boys (who are her friends)?

2. Do you insist that your girlfriend call you every day?

3. If your girlfriend doesn't walk with you between classes, does that make you upset?

4. Have you ever yelled or raised your voice at your girlfriend?

5. Have you ever hit or threatened to hit your girlfriend?

6. Do you get jealous when your girlfriend spends time with her friends and isn't hanging out with you?

7. Do you say mean or nasty things to your girlfriend if she doesn't hang out with you?

8. Have you ever made your girlfriend do something she said no to repeatedly?

*If you scored **less than 2**, your relationship is in good shape. If you scored **3–5**, then your relationship may not be healthy. If you scored **6–8**, then check yourself. You are not treating your girlfriend right. If you have concerns about your behavior, you may want to ask for help from a guidance counselor or another trusted adult.*

Sexually Transmitted Diseases (STDs)

When untreated, STDs can lead to infertility (the inability to father children) and even death. Here are the six most common STDs in men.

AIDS: A viral disease that attacks and wears down the immune system. Acquired immune deficiency syndrome (AIDS) is caused by the human immunodeficiency virus (HIV).

Chlamydia: An infection caused by the bacterium *Chlamydia trachomatis*.

Genital herpes: A viral infection caused by the herpes simplex virus (HSV) that can cause blisters and sores.

Gonorrhea: An infection caused by the bacterium *Neisseria gonorrhoeae*.

Human papillomavirus (HPV): A virus that can cause genital warts and increase the risk of various cancers.

Syphilis: An infection caused by the bacterium *Treponema pallidum*.

If you're in a serious relationship, it is also possible that your friends are influencing your decisions about having a physical relationship with your girlfriend. Even if your friends aren't pressuring you, you're getting the message from the media—whether TV, film, or Internet—which are saturated with images and stories focusing on sex and seduction. Studies have shown that teens exposed to heavy sexual content in the media are twice as likely to engage in a sexual relationship.

Any kind of sexual activity should be treated very seriously. Being sexually active can lead to all kinds of serious consequences—from pregnancy to sexually transmitted diseases (STDs) to emotional problems. Condoms are a form of contraception that can help prevent pregnancy as well as some STDs; however, they are not 100 percent effective. Be careful, and remember that the safest sex is abstinence—not having sex at all. If you need more information, you may want to speak to your parents, a health teacher or guidance counselor, a doctor, or another trusted adult.

In a good relationship, your girlfriend will understand and accept your values and beliefs. So make sure you talk to her about how you feel and why you feel that way. Remember, you have to make the choice to do what seems right to you.

CHAPTER EIGHT

Endings and Beginnings

Ben was devastated. His girlfriend of two years, Lucille, had just dumped him. They had started dating when they were in eighth grade. They would go to the park, watch movies, take walks, and play basketball. He had his first kiss with her. But recently, Lucille had started acting differently when she was around Ben. She didn't have time to stop to talk when he saw her in the hallway. And she often seemed irritated and angry with him. But yesterday was the worst—Lucille had texted him two fateful words: "It's over."

When Ben's girlfriend dumped him, it really hurt. And it hurt even more because she chose an unfair way to break up. Anyone who has been in a serious relationship with another person deserves to be told face-to-face when it's over. If the dumper hides behind technology, the dumpee not only feels rejected but insulted as well. His first thought is likely to be, "So that's how much our relationship meant to her?"

When she breaks up with you. The first thing to do is accept that the other person has reached a point in her life in which she's decided she doesn't want to date you anymore. People change. You can't control how your girl thinks about you after a few months or even years of being in a close relationship. If she doesn't feel the same way about you anymore, that doesn't mean you are worthless or that she is cruel. Change happens.

The second thing to do is to not hold on to false hope that she will change her mind and decide to come back. If she has reached the point of saying that it's over, it probably is. What you need to do is recognize that the best thing for you is to let go and move on.

When you break things off. When things don't feel right anymore, it could be time for you to end the relationship. While dealing with being dumped by

"The hottest love has the coldest end."
—Socrates

Some Reasons for Breaking Up

- She's cheated on you.
- She's disrespectful of you, often insulting you or putting you down.
- You've grown apart, and you no longer want to spend your time with her.
- You have different goals that won't allow you to stay together.

your girlfriend is hard, it can be just as challenging to break up with her. This requires you to be open and honest, while recognizing that you might be hurting her feelings.

Making the decision to break it off can be hard. In some cases, it may be as simple as not having strong feelings for your girlfriend. Or you recognize that there is something about her that you can't stand. Whatever the reason, it is in the best interest of both of you to end the relationship. There is no good reason to remain in a relationship that leaves both of you unhappy. Having to break up with someone, while difficult, will make you become a stronger person.

The best advice to follow when breaking up with a girl is to be sensitive. Think to yourself, "How would I like to be treated in this situation?" If you put yourself in the shoes of your girlfriend and have that attitude, you will be able to let her down easy and possibly become friends one day.

Other tips for a breakup include making sure that it is done in private. Don't dump her in a restaurant surrounded by a group of people. It could get ugly. But make sure that you break up with her to her face; don't use any kind of Internet messaging service or a text message. In the same way, breaking up over the phone, rather than face-to-face, is wrong.

Honesty is the best policy when breaking up with a girl. If you don't feel the same attraction you did for

Tips for Making a Clean Break

DO Give her a legitimate reason why you want to end the relationship.

DO Break up with her face-to-face.

DON'T Break up with her via text message, instant message, or e-mail.

DON'T Break up with her over the phone.

DON'T Come up with some flimsy excuse.

your girlfriend, the fair thing to do for her is to break up. Staying in a relationship with someone because she is still interested in you, but you really aren't, is unfair. Coming clean and letting her know why you think it needs to end is the only way to have a "good" breakup.

For the most part, breakups can be messy. In the worst-case scenario, you never talk to her again. Other cases may not be as bad, and you may end up becoming good friends.

Feeling depressed after a breakup. Whether it was your decision or hers, you can feel really sad after a breakup. The painful feelings of loss can overwhelm you with strong emotions, including anger, sorrow, grief, and depression.

However, be aware that if negative thoughts and feelings of depression persist for more than two weeks, you may be suffering from a mental disorder known as clinical depression. Its symptoms include feelings of extreme sadness and hopelessness, an inability to concentrate, feelings of guilt, and thoughts of death. Suicide among teens commonly occurs following a stressful life event—and that includes a breakup with a boyfriend or girlfriend. According to the Centers for Disease Control and Prevention, the third-leading cause of death among fifteen- to twenty-five-year-olds is suicide. In 2004, 82 percent of all suicides ages ten to twenty-four were boys.

If you're worried that a friend is depressed or possibly suicidal, you need to get help for that person. Share your concerns with an adult—your parents, a school counselor, your family doctor, or a religious leader. You could also contact a suicide prevention hotline—see the hotline telephone numbers listed on page 63.

Moving on and starting over. Moving on after a painful breakup can be a difficult process, especially if the breakup wasn't your idea. What's important is to try to stay strong and take care of yourself. Try to

Symptoms of Clinical Depression

- A loss of interest in activities previously enjoyed
- Feelings of worthlessness or guilt
- Fatigue or loss of energy
- Withdrawal from friends and family
- Sudden decline in grades
- Appetite or weight changes

eat well and get plenty of sleep. Go out for a run or get some other kind of exercise. There is nothing like a good run to take your mind off of something and help you feel good about yourself.

The time right after a breakup can be the hardest. Depending on how close you had grown to your ex-girlfriend, you may have a whole lot of free time. This can be both good and bad. Fill the hours by getting together with friends. Or pick up a new activity or hobby to help keep your mind off of her.

Push yourself to act like you're okay, even if you're feeling terrible. Try not to be hard on yourself. If she was the one who broke up with you, keep reminding yourself that the breakup was not your fault. It wasn't

Tips for Getting Over a Breakup

Take care of yourself physically: Get enough sleep, eat healthy foods, and exercise regularly.

Don't focus your thoughts on what happened: Don't just sit around the house and feel sorry for yourself. Instead, try to think about other possibilities in your life. Set new goals for yourself and your future.

Think about your good qualities: Getting dumped will leave your self-esteem at a new low. Take some time to think about or even write down some of your positive characteristics.

Do the things you normally enjoy: Go and enjoy a favorite activity, whether it's a sport or a good book. Hang out with some friends and try to forget the girl.

Share your feelings: Sit down with a trusted friend or with a parent and talk about what you are going through. It will feel good to get your problems off your chest.

Give yourself time: You won't get over the girl right away. Allow for time to heal your wounds.

something you said or did wrong. Sometimes, as people grow older, they realize they want something different in a relationship. There are other girls out there who will appreciate you. Stay positive and hold on to your self-respect and self-confidence.

Try to go through the motions during your day-to-day life, even though it can be hard. Keep telling yourself, "It's not the end of the world. Things will get better." In time, they really will get better. You just have to give yourself time.

Whatever you do, don't look to jump into a new relationship right way. Take some time off before trying to date someone again. But don't let that stop you from getting to know new people and making new friends. Eventually, you'll get over that old relationship and one of those new friends might begin to mean something special to you.

While romantic relationships can be one of the most challenging and confusing parts of life, they can also be the most rewarding. During the emotional highs and lows of crushes and romances, you have the chance to grow and learn how to be the best for yourself and for others.

Books

Hartman, Christie. *Changing Your Game: A Man's Guide to Success With Women.* Denver, Colo.: 5280 Press, 2012.

Langford, Jo. *The Sex EDcylopedia: A Comprehensive Guide to Healthy Sexuality, For the Modern, Male Teen.* Las Vegas Nev.: The Nazca Plains Corporation, 2011.

Marshall, Andrew G. *I Love You, But . . . I'm Not in Love With You.* Deerfield Beach, Fla.: Health Communications, Inc., 2010.

Internet Addresses

Teen Relationships
http://www.teenrelationships.org/

TeensHealth: Sexual Health
http://kidshealth.org/teen/sexual_health/

Hotlines

National Domestic Violence Hotline
1-800-799-SAFE (7233)

National Suicide Prevention Lifeline
1-800-273-TALK (8255)

INDEX

An Unloved Guy's Guide: How to Deal